This book is for Caitlin Purves

James T. de Kay is the author and illustrator of two adult books, *Stargazers* and *The Left-Handed Book*. His belief that "men make history" led to the writing of his first Step-Up Book, *Meet Christopher Columbus*. Martin Luther King, Jr., a man who changed history's course, inspired him to write a second. The father of a Step-Up age boy, Mr. de Kay lives with his wife and son in Irvington, New York.

This title was originally catalogued by the Library of Congress as follows: De Kay, James T. Meet Martin Luther King, by James T. de Kay. Illustrated with photos, and drawings by Ted Burwell. New York, Random House [1969] 89 p. ill ports. 22 cm. (Step-up books, SU19) A biography of the man largely responsible for uniting American Negroes in the f for civil rights. 1. King, Martin Luther—Juvenile literature. [1. King, Martin Luther] I. Burwell, Ted, illus. II. T E185.97.K5D43   323.4'0924   [B]   [92]   78-79789   ISBN: 0-394-80055-9   ISBN: 0-394-90055-3 (lib. bdg.)

Meet
Martin Luther King, Jr.

by James T. de Kay

Illustrated with photographs

and drawings by Ted Burwell

Step-Up Books — Random House
New York

1
Meet
Martin Luther King, Jr.

Martin Luther King, Jr. was a fighter. He fought people who used guns and bombs against him. But he did not use a gun. He fought with words and ideas. He believed words and ideas could beat guns.

He fought for fair laws. He fought for an end to hate. He fought for a better life for all Americans. Thousands of people knew he was right. Thousands followed him. And slowly America began to change.

Martin Luther King lost his life in the fight to change America. But his words and ideas fight on.

3

2
Big Words
and a Hard Head

When Martin Luther King, Jr. was born, he didn't yell like most babies. He lay very still. He was so quiet the doctor thought he was dead.

Smack! The doctor gave the fat baby a hard spank. At last Martin Luther King, Jr. gave his first cry.

The peaceful baby was born in Atlanta, Georgia, in January, 1929.

Martin Luther King, Jr. was a big name for a little boy. Everyone called him "M.L."

M.L.'s father's name was Martin Luther King, too. He was minister of the Ebenezer Baptist Church. On Sundays he spoke in church. He talked to the people about God, and tried to help them live good lives.

M.L.'s mother was Alberta King. She had been a teacher before her children were born. M.L. had an older sister, Christine, and a younger brother, Alfred Daniel.

The Kings lived in a comfortable house. They had nice clothes and plenty to eat. But M.L. grew up knowing that many people in Atlanta were poor and didn't have these things.

The church was a big part of M.L.'s life. As a tiny boy, he sang hymns there. He sang all by himself in front of hundreds of people.

And his father made him learn things from the Bible, the great book of the church.

M.L. and Christine and Alfred Daniel had to say their Bible verses out loud at dinner.

From the time he was a little boy, M.L. loved words. He loved to hear his father speak in church. He would watch the way people listened. He could see how strong words were. When he was little he said to his mother, "You just wait and see. I'm going to get me some big words."

M.L. loved to play, too. He was small for his age. But he played hard. Some of his friends thought he played too hard.

One time, when he was five, he was playing on the stairs. Suddenly he slipped and fell off. Crash!

He dropped 20 feet to the floor. He landed on his head and tumbled into the cellar. But he was not hurt!

Two other times cars smashed into his bicycle. Both times he was thrown to the ground. But he was not hurt either time.

Once he and his brother were playing baseball. His brother swung the bat hard. It slipped out of his hands and hit M.L. on the head. M.L. fell down, but he got right up. Once again he was not hurt!

Years later, Martin Luther King thought of all the times he was hit on the head. "God was looking out for me even then," he grinned. "He must have given me a hard head."

3

Jim Crow

M.L. was a happy little boy. But when he was about five, something happened that made him very sad.

Across the street from the Kings' house stood a small grocery store. Every day M.L. went over to play with the grocer's two little boys.

Then a strange thing happened. One day M.L. went to play as usual. But the boys didn't come out. Their mother came instead. She told M.L. to go home. She said her boys could never play with him again.

M.L. wanted to cry. He didn't understand. He ran home to his mother and asked what was wrong.

Mrs. King sighed and looked sad. She picked him up and put him on her lap. Then she began to explain.

She said everyone in the grocer's family had light skin. They were called "white" people. But everyone in M.L.'s family had dark skin. They were called "Negroes," or "black" people or "colored" people.

Then she said that some white people didn't like Negroes. She told him how, long, long ago, whites brought Negroes from Africa to America. They made them work in the fields as slaves. She told M.L. how cruel some white slave-owners were. They beat the Negroes with whips. They bought and sold them like cattle. They put them in chains.

Then came the Civil War. About 100 years ago, a great war was fought over the right to own slaves. After the war, the slaves were set free. But many whites still treated Negroes like slaves. They still beat them and whipped them. Sometimes they even killed them.

White people made special laws against Negroes. Some whites who didn't like Negroes called them "Jim Crows." So they called the special laws Jim Crow laws.

One Jim Crow law said no black child could go to school with white children. Another said Negroes could not eat in restaurants where white people ate. Negroes could not wash their clothes in the laundries white people used. They could not drink from the same fountains.

They could not sit next to white people in movie theaters. One law even told Negroes where to sit on buses. White people could sit anywhere. But Negroes had to sit in the back.

The laws kept black people and white people apart. This was called segregation.

M.L.'s mother told him not to think about the Jim Crow laws. They were bad laws. They made life hard. But he should never think whites were better than Negroes. "You are just as good as anyone," she said.

M.L.'s father hated the laws. He tried very hard to fight segregation. He would not ride Atlanta buses. He kept away from segregated stores.

One time he took M.L. to buy some shoes. They walked into a store and sat down near the front. A white salesman came over and told them to go to the back. The seats in the front were for white people.

M.L.'s father got very angry. He turned to the white man. "We'll either buy shoes sitting here, or we won't buy shoes at all!" he said. Then he took M.L. by the hand and marched out of the store.

M.L. never forgot how much his father hated the Jim Crow laws.

4

School Days

M.L. was small. But he was so smart his mother let him go to school a year early. Then one day he told his friends about his last birthday. "There were *five* candles on my cake," he said. His teacher heard him. She sent him home and told him to come back in a year.

When Martin came back, he did very well. He learned quickly. And he loved sports. It didn't matter that he was small. He played just as hard as the big boys.

He was fullback on the football team. He was on the basketball team. He wrestled anybody who wanted to fight, big or small.

Martin liked to dance. He also liked to dress well. His high school friends called him "Tweed," because he wore tweed clothes.

And he still loved words. Reading was easy for him. He got so far ahead of his class that he skipped the ninth and twelfth grades.

Martin used words in many ways.

Sometimes he could win fights by talking instead of by hitting.

And he could speak in front of many people. He practiced his talks in front of a mirror. When he was 15, he won a big speaking contest in Atlanta.

One time Martin and some other students went to a speaking contest out of town. It was a long trip. On the way back, the bus was filled with people. But the boys found seats at last.

Then some white people got on. The bus driver turned around. He told Martin and the other Negroes to stand up and give their seats to the white people. That was the law.

Martin and his friends knew this was unfair. Why should they give their seats to someone else? They had paid just as much for the ride. They did not move. This made the bus driver very angry. He yelled at them. He called them awful names.

Martin's teacher was there. She told the boys they had to obey the law. So they stood up and let white people take their seats. Martin was furious. He had to stand for about two hours. He had never been so angry in his life. It was hard not to hate all white people.

Now Martin hated the Jim Crow laws as much as his father did. But what could he do to fight them?

5

Gandhi's Way

At 15, Martin passed a hard exam. He got into Morehouse College, in Atlanta. His father and grandfather had both gone there. It was the college of many famous Negro men.

Martin went to classes every day. He heard important men speak.

At high school Martin had planned to be a doctor. He had not wanted to be a minister like his father. But at Morehouse he changed his mind.

People listened when a minister spoke. Maybe as a minister he could do more to help the black people.

Martin's father was pleased. But he didn't tell Martin. He asked him to speak in the church to see how well he could do. It was Martin's first sermon. He was only 17.

Martin began to speak in the small room of the church. More and more people crowded in to hear him. Soon everyone had to move to the big hall.

Martin gave a very good speech. His father was very proud.

In the summer Martin worked. But he did not get jobs that paid well. He loaded trains and trucks. He did hard work in factories. These were the jobs most black men did. Martin wanted to live the hard life of Negro working men. Maybe he could see a way to make life better for them.

After Morehouse, Martin went to a special college for ministers. It was called Crozer. It was in the state of Pennsylvania.

There were no Jim Crow laws in Pennsylvania. At Crozer Martin went to school with white people for the first time. He liked some of them very much. He saw that there were different kinds of white people.

An important thing happened to Martin at Crozer. He learned about Mohandas Gandhi, a great leader of India. Like Martin, Gandhi had lived under cruel and unfair laws. But he and his people found a way to fight these laws. They simply broke them. When the police threw them in jail, they didn't fight back. Soon the jails of India were filled. There was no one left to do the work. At last the leaders had to change the laws to get the country going again. Gandhi had won! And he had won without hurting or killing people.

Martin read more and more about Gandhi. Could Gandhi's way work against the Jim Crow laws?

6
Three Choices

Martin was the best student at Crozer. When he graduated, he won money to go to another college.

He chose Boston University, in Massachusetts. He wanted to study the ideas of great men. He would read what they had said about how people should live.

Martin and his friends liked to talk about these ideas. They met for coffee in Martin's apartment.

Soon many black students in Boston were coming there to talk. They became a club. They talked of ways to make life better for Negroes.

Martin had many friends, black and white, in Boston. But he had no favorite girl. Then a friend told him of a lovely girl named Coretta Scott. She was studying to be a singer. He called and made a date.

The day they met, Martin could not stop looking at Coretta. He thought she was very beautiful. He began to tell her some of his ideas. They talked and talked.

Later on Martin turned to Coretta. "You're everything I'm looking for in a wife," he said.

Martin and Coretta fell in love. Soon he asked her to marry him.

It was hard for Coretta to decide. She was a very good singer. She had planned to sing in concerts all over the country. If she married, she might have to give up her singing. She wondered if she loved Martin enough to do it. The answer was yes.

That summer, Martin and Coretta were married in Alabama.

Martin and Coretta finished their studies in Boston. It was time to decide what to do. They had many friends in Boston. They had Negro friends and white friends. And Boston was in the North, where there were no Jim Crow laws. Life might be better for them there.

Some churches in the North asked Martin to be their minister. It would be nice to live in the North. But Martin said no. He wanted to help the Negroes. The place to start was in the South, where life was hardest for them.

Martin took a job with the Dexter Avenue Church. It was in the city of Montgomery, in Alabama.

The Kings moved to Montgomery. They settled in a big white house near the Dexter Avenue Church.

On Sundays Martin spoke at the church and Coretta sang in the choir. Martin visited the sick. He helped the poor. Soon he was an important leader in Montgomery.

Montgomery was a segregated city like Atlanta. There were lots of Jim Crow laws. Whites and blacks went to different schools. They rode in different taxis. They went to different churches. Martin met with Negroes who wanted to fight against segregation. They talked about taxis and about schools. But most of all, they talked about the city buses.

All bus riders, black and white, paid at the front door. But often only the whites could sit down.

All the drivers were white. Some of them made the Negroes climb off the bus after they paid. The Negroes had to walk to the rear door and climb back on. Only then could they sit down. And if white people wanted the seats in the back, the Negroes could not sit down at all.

The drivers treated Negroes like animals. Sometimes they called them "niggers," and other terrible names.

The Negroes hated to ride the city buses. But they had to get to work. What else could they do?

7

Rosa Parks

On December 1, 1955, a woman named Rosa Parks did something about the Jim Crow buses.

Mrs. Parks was a Negro. She worked in a department store. That evening she climbed on a bus and sat down.

Each time the bus stopped, more people got on. Soon no seats were left in the white part of the bus.

At the next stop some white people got on. The driver got up and walked over to Mrs. Parks. He told her to give her seat to a white woman.

But Rosa Parks was tired. Her feet hurt. She did something she had never done before. She just stayed in her seat.

Again the driver told Mrs. Parks to get up. But she would not move.

The driver was furious. He called a policeman. He told him that Mrs. Parks would not give up her seat.

When the policeman heard this, he pulled Mrs. Parks off the bus.

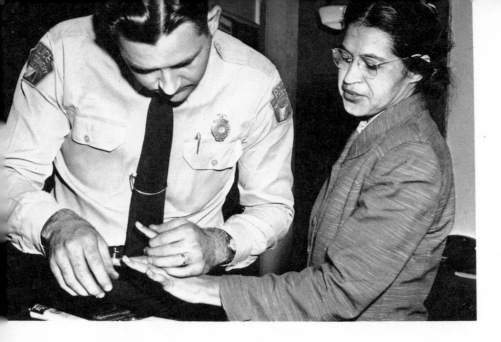

He took her to the police station.
The police took her fingerprints and
threw her in jail. All because she
was tired and didn't want to get up!

Negroes all over the city heard
about Rosa Parks. They were very
angry. They were mad at the Jim
Crow laws. They were mad at the
police. They were mad at the bus
company. But what could they do?

Then one man said, "Why don't we boycott the buses?" This meant that all the Negroes would stop riding the buses. Soon the bus company would lose money. Maybe then the owners would be fair to Negroes.

Boycott! The word spread like wild-fire. Someone called Martin Luther King. He liked the idea right away.

But a boycott would work only if all the Negroes stayed off the buses. How could the leaders get word to every Negro in Montgomery in time?

Martin and the others worked fast. They wrote a letter about the boycott. They gave copies away in every part of the city where Negroes lived. But they could not reach everybody.

Could they reach enough to make the boycott work?

Then they had some good luck. A Negro maid got a copy of the letter. She could not read well. So she showed it to the white woman she worked for. The woman read the note. It made her angry. She didn't want the Negroes to boycott the buses. She called the Montgomery newspaper and told the editor about the boycott.

The editor of the paper was white, too. He got just as angry. He wrote a story saying the boycott was bad. The story was printed in the paper.

Many Negroes who did not get the note saw the story in the paper.

The paper was against the boycott. But it helped to make it work!

The night before the boycott, the Kings were up late. Their new baby, Yolanda, was crying. At last she was quiet. But her parents stayed awake worrying about tomorrow. Would the boycott work?

Morning came. Coretta looked out the window at the bus stop. Soon the first bus of the day rolled up. On most days it was filled with Negroes.

"Martin! Martin! Come quickly!" Coretta cried. Martin ran to the window. The bus was empty! He wanted to shout with joy.

Another empty bus drove by. And then another! The boycott was on!

8

The Boycott Gets a Leader

All day long empty buses rolled through the streets of Montgomery. Black people all over the city joined the boycott. Some walked to work. Some rode on mules or in wagons. Some rode bicycles. Each fought the Jim Crow laws in his own way.

Later that day, the men who planned the boycott had a meeting. Martin Luther King was elected president of the group. The group would be called the Montgomery Improvement Association, or MIA.

That night King went to a big meeting in a church. Thousands of Negroes crowded inside and outside the church. They wanted to know what would happen.

Should the boycott go on? It was hard to walk to work. It was hard to ride a mule to the store. But it was the only way to fight the Jim Crow laws. The people voted. Those who wanted to keep the boycott going were asked to stand.

All through the crowded church people rose to their feet.

They looked around them. Every person in the room was on his feet! All the Negroes wanted to stay off the buses. A great cheer went up.

The boycott would go on!

Martin Luther King stood up to speak. He knew he must speak well. Black people in Montgomery were doing a brave and dangerous thing. And they trusted him to lead them.

"There comes a time when people get tired," he said. "We are here this evening to say we are tired of being kicked about."

Everyone cheered wildly. The bus boycott would go on. And the boycott had a leader!

9

The Whites Get Tough

The boycott went straight through December and into January. Black people still walked. They still rode mules and shared cars.

People all over the country sent money to help the black people of Montgomery. Soon Martin and the MIA rounded up hundreds of cars.

The Negroes began to drive each other to work in "car pools."

Now white people in Montgomery were angry. The men who ran the bus company were furious. They were losing money. They wanted the boycott stopped. The mayor hated it. He told the police to get tough with the boycott leaders.

The police got tough. And the first person they were tough with was Martin Luther King, Jr.

One day Martin was driving his car slowly down the street. All at once two white policemen stopped him. "Get out, King," they said. "You're under arrest for driving 30 miles an hour in a 25 mile zone."

Martin knew they were wrong. But he had to obey. They pushed him in their car and drove him to jail.

The news spread fast. Soon a large crowd of angry Negroes had gathered outside the jail. The jailer was afraid they might break in. He set King free. But King would not stay out long. Again and again the police thought of reasons to arrest him.

The police were not the only ones who tried to stop King. One night Martin spoke at a meeting. Coretta stayed home talking to a friend. In the back room little Yoki slept.

A car roared past the house. A man in the car threw something out. Coretta heard a loud thump on the porch. She thought someone must have thrown a brick. But she was worried. She led her friend to the back of the house.

Just then there was an explosion! It was a bomb! It had blown a big hole in the porch. Many of the front windows were broken. But no one was hurt.

Someone rushed to tell Martin.

Soon a crowd of angry Negroes stood in front of the house. They wanted to kill the people who threw the bomb. White policemen drove up and told all the blacks to go home. But the blacks would not move. They wanted a fight. When the mayor came, the crowd muttered in anger.

King arrived. By now more than a thousand blacks were there. As he pushed through the crowd, he heard a Negro say to a policeman, "Let's battle it out!" A terrible fight was about to begin.

Martin stood on his ruined porch. He spoke to the black people.

"Don't get panicky," he said. "If you have weapons, take them home."

"We must meet our white brothers' hate with love," he said. He told them others would try to stop him. But still black people must fight on for freedom. "If I am stopped, our work will not stop. For what we are doing is right!"

"God bless you, son!" someone cried. Slowly, the crowd broke up.

The Negroes were amazed. Someone had tried to kill Martin Luther King, but he had talked of love. And the police were amazed. "I owe my life to that nigger preacher," said one of them.

10
Victory

It was March. The battle of the buses dragged on.

The white leaders of Montgomery decided to try something new. They had the boycott leaders arrested for stopping the bus company's business.

Martin Luther King went to court. He was found guilty and fined $500. But he didn't mind. Money would come from somewhere. He knew his fight could not be stopped.

And so did his people. A big crowd cheered him as he left the court. "Long live the King!" they cried.

Eight months later, Martin Luther King sat in court again. It was November 13, 1956. White leaders had a new plan. They said the MIA car pool took business from the bus company. They asked the judge to say the car pool was against the law.

King was worried. It looked as if the judge would make the MIA give up the car pool. Then the boycott would have to end. The black people would have to ride Jim Crow buses again. The fight would be lost!

King sat sadly in court. Suddenly a reporter handed him a note. It was exciting news from the United States Supreme Court. This is the most important court in America.

What it says is more important than what state courts say. And now the Supreme Court had said segregation in city buses was against the law!

King could hardly believe it. The Negroes had won! Jim Crow buses were gone forever from Montgomery.

On December 21, 1956, King stood at a bus stop with other boycott leaders. Soon a bus pulled up.

As Martin Luther King climbed on, the driver said, "We're glad to have you this morning." King smiled and walked to a seat near the front.

11 SCLC

Blacks had beaten Jim Crow in one city. Why not in others?

Martin Luther King, Jr. and other Negro ministers of the South met in Atlanta. They formed a new group to fight segregation. It was called the Southern Christian Leadership Conference, or SCLC. And Martin Luther King was elected president.

In speech after speech, he told Negroes how to fight. He told them not to obey unfair laws. He said to go to places Jim Crow laws said not to go, and do things the laws said not to do. If police came to take them to jail, they should go quietly. Even if people hurt them, they must hurt no one. "We must have the courage to refuse to fight back," he said. "We must use the weapon of love." He believed white leaders would get tired of all the trouble and change the laws. Gandhi had won this way.

SCLC had other work. All over the South, whites kept blacks from voting. Negroes couldn't elect their leaders, or even vote for President.

This was unfair. In America everyone should have the right to vote. Now SCLC would fight to bring that right to five million black Americans.

SCLC had sent out its battle cry. A peaceful war against segregation had begun.

For two years King led the voting drive. He ran meetings and gave speeches. He wrote a book about the boycott. And still he kept up his work at the Dexter Avenue Church.

Martin Luther King loved all the people of his church. He had shared a great struggle with the Negroes of Montgomery. His daughter Yolanda and his son Martin Luther King III had been born in Montgomery.

But he knew it was time to move on.

One Sunday when church was over, King asked everyone to stay. He told them he must leave. He must have more time to work for SCLC. Black people all over America needed his help. He had become the leader of their fight for freedom. He would go to Atlanta and work in his father's church.

The people were very sad. They hated to let their great minister go. But they knew it was right.

At the end he asked them to join hands and sing a hymn with him. And as the music filled the church he loved, Martin Luther King broke down and cried.

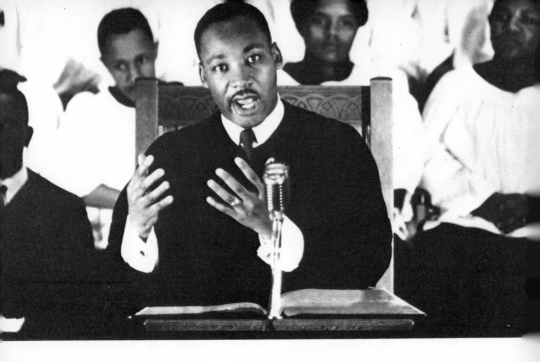

12   The Sit-Ins

From Ebenezer Baptist Church in
Atlanta, King spoke out to Negroes
everywhere. He called them to fight
for their freedom. He gave them
hope. He gave them courage. Soon
many Negroes took up the fight
against segregation in America.

One afternoon in February, 1959, four black teenagers marched into a Woolworth's store in Greensboro, North Carolina. Quietly they sat down at the Jim Crow lunch counter. They asked to buy food.

The white people in the store were shocked and angry. The waitress would not serve them. Other whites shouted bad names at them.

But the young Negroes pretended not to hear. They just sat quietly.

The next day they came back again. Still they were not served. So they came back still another day. They said they would keep coming back until they were served.

And that is how "sit-ins" began.

Soon blacks started sit-ins in 14 other cities.

Many whites hated the sit-ins. They tried to stop them. They beat the blacks. They spat on them. They burned them with cigarettes.

But day after day the blacks came back. And at last some of the Jim Crow stores gave up. They agreed to let Negroes eat at their counters.

The young blacks had won another great battle against Jim Crow.

In October, 1960, King and a large group held a sit-in at a big Atlanta store. The store would not serve them food. Soon the police came. They arrested over 50 people. And that night, once again, Martin Luther King slept behind bars.

13 Freedom Rides

After the sit-ins came "Freedom Rides." In the South, some of the big buses traveling from state to state were still segregated. Freedom Rides were sit-ins on these buses.

On May 4, 1961, two Greyhound buses left Washington, D.C. They headed south. Thirteen freedom riders were on board. At every stop they sat at lunch counters marked "whites only." They used "white" waiting rooms. And on the buses, they always sat near the front.

What would happen? All over the country people waited for the news.

The trip began quietly. Then, at a stop in Alabama, some white people cut the tires of the first bus. They followed the bus out of town.

Soon the tires went flat. When the bus stopped, the white people set it on fire. As the frightened riders ran out, the whites attacked them.

The group had to give up the trip. Another group took over. But soon they, too, were attacked.

The next night the freedom riders held a huge meeting in a church in Montgomery. Martin Luther King rushed to Montgomery to speak.

While he spoke, a crowd of angry white people tried to break into the church. King asked his people to sing the black freedom song, "We Shall Overcome." As stones and bottles hit the church, the Negroes inside sang, "We are not afraid." At last soldiers sent the crowd home.

In the next days, a new group was set up to plan freedom rides. King was one of the leaders.

For months they planned rides and sent them off. And at last, the U.S. government sent out an order. It said segregation in all buses, trains and waiting rooms was against the law. The freedom riders had won!

King had a plan. Sit-ins at lunch counters and on buses had worked. Why not a sit-in for a whole city?

In December, 1961, freedom riders were arrested in Albany, Georgia. King began a great sit-in in Albany. For months he led marches. He led sit-ins all over the city. But somehow nothing happened. White leaders didn't change the laws. The black people gave up. It was the first time Martin Luther King had lost a fight.

14 Birmingham

Martin Luther King did not win in Albany. But he learned something there. He learned he could not fight a whole city with only a few hundred people. He needed an army.

He needed thousands of blacks to march against Jim Crow. He needed thousands who were not afraid to go to jail. And still more thousands to keep marching. He would show the whole country how much black people hated segregation. He would make white leaders see that they had to end the Jim Crow laws.

Where would he find such an army? Where would he fight his next battle? He picked Birmingham, Alabama. Birmingham was known as the worst Jim Crow city in America.

In April, 1963, King led a group of 40 marchers toward city hall. They would demand to talk to white leaders.

On they came. A thousand blacks lined the street shouting "Freedom has come to Birmingham!"

The police were waiting. Their chief was a fat, tough white man named Bull Connor. He made life hard for the Negroes of Birmingham.

Bull Connor watched the marchers coming. "Stop 'em!" he shouted. The police moved in. They rounded the marchers up and threw them in jail.

Whenever King was put in jail, he called Coretta right away. But this time he did not call. Two days passed. Coretta was very worried.

Then, at last, a call came. It was from John F. Kennedy, the President of the United States.

"I wanted you to know," he said, "that I have talked with Birmingham. I have arranged for your husband to call you." He told her that Martin was all right. It was wonderful news for Coretta.

Soon King was out of jail and out marching again. Each day more marched with him. And each day the police got tougher. They beat the blacks with clubs. They used fierce police dogs to attack the marchers.

They turned fire hoses on them. The water hit like a hammer. It was so strong it smashed the marchers to the ground.

Then King decided on a dangerous plan. There would be a children's march. He didn't think police could be cruel enough to attack children.

On a morning in May, the black children of Birmingham gathered on the streets. They began to march. And as they marched, they sang, "Deep in my heart, I do believe that we shall overcome some day."

Connor's police blocked off the street. They waited. The children began to run toward them. Then the police hit them with everything they had—hoses, dogs, clubs. They packed a thousand children off to jail. Some were only six years old.

The blacks of Birmingham could hardly believe it. What kind of men could put a six-year-old in jail? They rose in fury. Now thousands upon thousands marched against segregation in Birmingham.

The men who ran the city could take it no longer. On Friday, May 10, they met with Negro leaders. They promised to end the Jim Crow laws. Freedom had come to Birmingham!

15

"I Have a Dream"

All over America, Negroes watched
the news from Birmingham. They
said, "If blacks are brave enough
to march in Birmingham, we can
march too."

Now blacks marched everywhere.

All that long, hot summer of 1963 the crowds grew bigger. Where once there were hundreds of marchers, now there were thousands. Where once there were thousands, now there were hundreds of thousands.

In over 800 cities they marched and sang. They marched for the end of unfair laws. They shouted for the end of segregation. They cried out for freedom from coast to coast.

And then on August 28, Martin Luther King and other black leaders marched right into Washington, D.C. 250,000 people followed. They came from all over the country. They came by train and plane. They came by bus, by car, and even on foot.

Most of the crowd was Negro. But there were thousands of whites. They wanted to show that they hated segregation, too. They wanted to join the fight for freedom.

It was not an angry crowd. The people were proud and happy. They sang songs and listened to speeches.

Many black leaders gave fine speeches. But, at the end of the day, Martin Luther King gave a speech America will never forget.

"I have a dream today!" His voice shook with feeling. Some day, he said, "little black boys and black girls will join hands with little white boys and white girls and walk together as sisters and brothers.

"I have a dream today!"

A cheer went up from the crowd.

Some day, King went on, *all* God's children would join hands. Together they would sing the old Negro song, "Free at last, free at last. Thank God Almighty, we are free at last!"

When he finished, many of the marchers were crying. They stood and cheered Martin Luther King. Then everyone joined hands, blacks and whites together, and sang "We Shall Overcome."

16

The Nobel Prize

Martin Luther King was a famous man. He spoke and worked all around the country. But he tried to be with his family as much as he could.

Mrs. King worked in the fight for freedom, too. Whenever she could, she marched by her husband's side.

The Kings had four children now. There were two boys, Martin and Dexter, and two girls, Yolanda and Bernice. They loved to play with their father. They would rough-house with him in the living room.

Martin Luther King was often in jail. This was hard for the children to understand. "Your daddy went to jail to help people," Mrs. King once said. Soon after, Yolanda heard on television that her father was in jail again. She burst into tears. "Don't cry, Yoki," said little Martin. "Daddy's gone to help *more* people."

The most important prize in the world is the Nobel Peace Prize awarded by the country of Norway. Each year it is given to the person who has done the most for peace.

In October, 1964, the Norwegian government sent out an exciting announcement. Martin Luther King had won the Nobel Prize!

The Kings flew over to Norway to accept the prize. It was a medal and $54,000. King would give the money to several Negro groups. He said it belonged to all American Negroes.

He made a speech thanking the Norwegians. He said the prize was not just for him, but for "all men who love peace and brotherhood."

Then the Kings traveled around Europe. They met important people. Crowds cheered them. But soon they left for home. They had work to do.

17
Selma and the North

Martin Luther King stopped to rest his feet. He was leading 650 people on a long, hard march from Selma, Alabama, to Montgomery, the state capital.

For weeks King had been working for fair voting laws in Selma. A young black working with him had been shot by a policeman. King had called on his people to march. They would show that blacks would risk their lives for the right to vote.

Many ministers and white people from the North had joined the march.

King knew the march would be dangerous. "I can't promise that it won't get you beaten," he told his people. "I can't promise that it won't get your house bombed. But we must stand up for what is right."

It was a 50-mile march. Twice the marchers had tried to get through. Police met them on the road with whips. They knocked them down and trampled them with their horses.

Then Lyndon Johnson, the new American President, sent soldiers to protect the marchers. But two would never march again. A young Northern minister was beaten to death by Alabama whites. And later a white woman was shot and killed.

But the others marched on, mile by mile. And at last, on March 25, 1965, they reached Montgomery. There King spoke to his people. How long would they have to wait for freedom? "Not long," he said. "Because no lie can live forever." And segregation was a lie.

Soon after, the U.S. government passed a voting rights bill. Millions of blacks could vote at last!

Now King turned north. He began to work in the city of Chicago.

There were no Jim Crow laws in Northern cities. But Negroes still had problems. Many whites would not rent rooms to Negroes. And most blacks were poor. So they had to live in "slums." In Chicago over 800,000 blacks lived in row upon row of dirty buildings. There were rats and bugs. Often there was no heat.

King helped blacks to form groups. Now they could make owners clean up the buildings and give them heat.

He led many marches for "open housing." At last Chicago leaders signed a paper. It said owners could not refuse to rent rooms to Negroes.

Now King carried the fight to other cities in the North.

18

Tired of Waiting

Martin Luther King had carried the fight around the country. And slowly life was getting better for Negroes all over America.

But now he faced a new problem. This time it did not come from whites. It came from other blacks.

In August, 1965, California blacks had exploded into a rioting mob.

Soon Negroes in other American cities did the same. Crowds of angry blacks broke into stores and stole things. They set fire to buildings, yelling, "Burn, baby, burn!" When police couldn't stop them, soldiers had to be called in. About 150 people were killed, and thousands hurt. A wave of fear swept over the country.

The Negroes were sick and tired of waiting for a better life. They were tired of slums and Jim Crow, tired of bad jobs and poor pay. And they were tired of hearing Martin Luther King asking them to be patient.

Blacks had been stoned, bombed and shot to death in the fight for freedom. Shouldn't they fight back?

Now many Negroes listened to new leaders, younger and louder then King. They said the answer was "Black Power." Negroes should stick together to be strong. Some wanted to break away and start a new country. Others wanted to fight white men with guns and bombs.

The angry leaders upset King. If blacks followed them, there would be killings and burnings all over the country. There might even be war.

King knew it was hard for blacks to wait for freedom. He knew it took a long time to change bad laws. He agreed that America wasn't changing fast enough. But he asked his people not to kill to get what they wanted.

Fight harder, he said—but in a new way. Money is green. "Green Power— that's the kind of power we need," he said. "What good does it do to be able to eat at a lunch counter if you can't buy a hamburger?"

With more money, Negroes could have better houses and clothes and food. They could live better lives.

King began to plan a new march on Washington, a Poor People's March. The poor would demand better jobs and more pay. And the march would not just be for blacks. It would be for *all* poor people, white and black.

Now the poor asked King for help. He went to Memphis, Tennessee, to help garbagemen fight for more pay.

19

"I've Been to the Mountaintop"

A month before he went to Memphis, Martin Luther King spoke at Ebenezer. People had tried to kill him. He knew he might die any day. So today he talked of his own death. If he were to die, what should be said at his funeral? He told his people that his prizes were not important. His schools were not important. What mattered was how he had lived his life.

"I'd like somebody to mention that day," he said, "that Martin Luther King, Jr. tried to give his life serving others."

Now, in Memphis, 6,000 people marched behind Martin Luther King. They would show the whole country that the peaceful way still worked.

All at once young blacks near by began to smash windows and steal things. Soon a terrible riot began.

King's men rushed him to safety. The next day he left Memphis.

He was sad and upset. Had the riot been his fault? He asked, "Am I doing any good?" He was afraid a few black leaders might make more people riot. How could he stop them?

He might go on a "fast." He would stop eating to show black people how he felt about riots and angry talk. Then perhaps they would listen to his call for peace.

Then King and his men knew what to do. On the way to the Poor People's March, they would go back to Memphis. They would show they could win the fight *their* way.

Suddenly King wasn't worried any more. He knew black people would be free one day. Hating and killing would stop, and peace would come.

On April 3, 1968, he returned to Memphis. That night a great rain poured on the city. King went out into the storm to speak at a church.

Memphis whites talked of killing him, but he wasn't afraid. He called them "our sick white brothers." "Like anybody, I'd like to live a long life," he said. But it didn't matter now. Ahead he saw a time of peace, the "Promised Land" of the Bible. "I've been to the mountaintop," he said. "And I've seen the Promised Land. I may not get there with you. But...we as a people will get to the Promised Land. So I'm happy tonight. I'm not fearing any man."

A night later, King stood on his motel porch. At a window across the way, a shadow moved. Suddenly a shot rang out! King fell to the floor. Within an hour he was dead.

20

"Drum Major for Justice"

All over the world, people wept. Thousands came to the funeral in Atlanta. There were governors and senators, mayors, and judges of the Supreme Court. Black and white, rich and poor, young and old, they came to say good-by to a great man.

In some way, Martin Luther King had helped them all. He had helped the poor and the sick. He had made black people really believe they were "as good as anyone." And he had helped to wake up white Americans. He showed them that people all over their country were still not free.

He showed that they, too, must work for fair laws and fight for peace.

He didn't care about money or fame. He didn't even think his Nobel Prize was important. To him, justice was important. He called himself "a drum major for justice."

And laws were important. But only if they were fair laws. He went to jail 30 times fighting unfair laws.

Martin Luther King dreamed that one day black children and white would join hands as sisters and brothers. He did not live to see his dream come true. But he had looked down from the mountaintop and seen the Promised Land. And he had shown Americans a way to get there.